TRUE or FALSE?

Written by Susan McCloskey
Illustrated by Kersti Frigell

True or false?

Bees buzz when they are mad.

False!

Bees' wings buzz all the time.

True or false?

Bugs are always small.

False!

Some bugs are very big.

True or false?

Elephants are too big to run.

False!

Elephants can run very fast.

True or false?

Lizards always stay the same color.

False!

Some lizards can turn yellow, white, brown, or black.

True or false?

Cockroaches eat only what people eat.

False!

Cockroaches even eat glue.

True or false?

Dinosaurs were the biggest animals that ever lived.

False!

The blue whale is bigger than the biggest dinosaur.

True or false?

Crickets use their mouths to chirp.

Here's a clue: If you see a cricket,
look at its wings.